Contents

In the book «Norway» we have devided the country into 9 main areas. The photographs provide examples from mountain and coasts, from busy cities and wilderness - all year round.

Norway

"Ja, vi elsker dette landet ..." "Yes, we love this country ..." This is how Norway's national anthem begins. The anthem is a song of praise to Norway: the nation far to the north with its magnificent, wild, and – not least – incredibly varied scenery.

Its beauty ranges from the dramatic fjord landscapes of Western Norway to the luxuriant and fertile agricultural areas of Eastern Norway and Trøndelag; and to enchanting Northern Norway and Lofoten with its wealth of fish, its idyllic fishing villages situated below mighty, precipitous mountains.

There is just as much of a contrast between the island idyll of the south coast with its boating and swimming activities, and Pasvik in Finnmark, the western point of the Russian taiga (a continuous belt of conifer forest from Finnmark to Mongolia). Norway is thus, above all, a country of contrasts: a new landscape is revealed around the next corner.

Nature and the climate have formed those who live in this country. Through the centuries, cultural impulses from Europe and the rest of the world have been brought home and processed, and have provided their own Norwegian cultural impressions. For this reason, outsiders today still perceive Norway as an exotic and different country. This is despite the fact that modern Norway is considered one of the wealthiest and most developed countries in the world.

With its 387,000 square kilometres (nearly 150,000 square miles) Norway is the fifth largest country in Europe. This means that the 4.2 million Norwegians who live here have plenty of space in which to frolic, compared with the densely populated countries further south on the Continent.

Norway was united for the first time by the Viking king Harald Hårfagre in 872, and was an independent kingdom until 1319, when the male line of the Norwegian royal family died out. In the centuries that followed, Norway tempted a changing history as a dependency under Denmark, and then under Sweden. In 1814 Norway acquired its own constitution, and from 1905 it had its own king and flag.

Norway - the scenery and the people – is difficult to describe in words alone. Therefore, experience a unique journey through the book **"Norway – what a country!"**.

Enjoy yourself!

Oslo

HISTORICAL

Oslo was founded by Harald Hardråde in about 1048. Early on, the city became the cathedral city and trading centre for Østlandet. Oslo was made the capital for the first time in 1299. After the dissolution of the union with Denmark in 1814, it became the capital, where the king, Storting (parliament) and government were based. Today, Oslo is a national and international centre for art and culture.

Oslo – capital of Norway. A green and exciting town, it has the fascinating culture and open-air life of a metropolis and the picturesque charm of a small town: from the green hills with the world-famous sports arenas that surround the town to the busy open harbour with commercial vessels and pleasure craft as far as the eye can see. And at the harbour you can taste possibly the world's best shrimps.

THE MUSEUM CITY

With 40 to 50 small and large museums, Oslo ranks as one of Scandinavia's foremost museum cities. Here you can experience everything from Norwegian folklore, Viking culture and Edvard Munch's world-famous paintings to Gustav Vigeland's unique sculpture park.

May 17 – Norway's national day. This is first and foremost a day of festivities for children. In their best clothes they walk in the children's procession to celebrate Norway as a free and independent country.

From the Palace balcony in Oslo, the Royal Family receives the people's tribute.

The children's procession in the street of Karl Johans gate is a spectacle without parallel. Children from a hundred schools advance up the hill to greet the royal family.

Holmenkollen – Oslo's famous ski arena. The atmosphere is almost magical when 100,000 spectators crowd on the slopes and around the outrun to cheer the ski jumpers in their daring leaps at Holmenkollen.

It is not unusual for tots of just three or four years to take part in children's skiing races. Here it is more important to have fun than to get ahead quickly...

In summer, the Holmenkollen skiing arenas are used for concerts, among other things.

The Vigeland
sculptures in the
Frogner park are the
masterpiece of sculptor
Gustav Vigeland
(1875 – 1943).
The enormous
collection portrays a
world of people and
animals sculpted in
stone, iron and
bronze.

The Munch Museum in
Oslo has the largest
collection of the works of
Edvard Munch (1875 -
1943). Here is perhaps
his most well-known
painting, "The Scream"
in the National Gallery.

The Oslo card is a "go as you please" card providing inexpensive access to museums and public transport as well as discounts on cinema tickets and guided tours in Oslo.

The 22 metre (72 ft) Oseberg ship, built in about 850 AD, in the Viking Ship Museum.

→ Evening mood at Akershus Fort, with the training ship Christian Radich in the foreground. The fort and castle were built by Håkon V in the year 1299.

In the Kon-Tiki Museum at Bygdøy you can see the Kon-Tiki raft on which ethnologist Thor Heyerdahl crossed the Pacific Ocean in 1947.

Eastern Norway

The paddle steamer Skibladner, "The White Swan of the Mjøsa", built in 1856. The Skibladner still sails on the Mjøsa, and is the world's oldest ship in regular service.

Østlandet includes eight of Norway's 19 counties. Geographically, the region covers the south-eastern part of Norway from the Swedish border in the east to Hardangervidda in the west. In the north, Østlandet borders Dovrefjell, while the Skagerak strait forms the southern border.

THE CONSTITUTION'S FOREFATHERS

The Eidsvoll building is the very symbol of Norway as a free and independent nation. Here, Norway's constitution was proclaimed on May 17, 1814. Today, the building is a museum where you can see the hall in which the national assembly was held in the spring of 1814.

Garmo Stave Church from the 13th century is one of the great attractions of the Sandvig Collection (De Sandvigste Samlingene) at Maihaugen, Lillehammer.

Folk dancing performance.

The Winter Olympics in 1994 were a great success for Norway and Lillehammer – both the sport and the event. The scene is from the closing ceremony on 12 February 1994.

Traditional agriculture using a horse and cart at Maihaugen.

Frederikstad's Old Town, from the 18th century, is the only fort town that has been preserved in Scandinavia. The town is surrounded by ramparts. Here is one of the gateways towards the river, Glomma.

Fredriksten Fort at Halden is one of the most prominent fort constructions in Norway.
The fort was built in 1644 – 45 in defence against the Swedes.

In Drøbak on the Oslo Fjord, shipping has been the main industry throughout the ages. So it is perhaps not so strange that even one of the houses is decorated with a figurehead.

Many people call Norway "the green belt of Europe" because of its clean environment. Østlandet is an eldorado for moose and other wild deer. The region also has a flourishing colony of bears, close to the Swedish border.

→

The Telemark Canal is considered the most beautiful canal construction in Europe.

Southern Norway

$\mathcal{M}$ost Norwegians associate Sørlandet with summer, sun and swimming. And it is not without cause that the population of Norway's two southernmost counties doubles during the summer season. With its idyllic skerries and picturesque small towns, the southern coast of Norway is a magnet for boating tourists.

FARMING TRADITIONS

But Sørlandet is more than skerries, attractive wooden houses painted white, and salt sea. Setesdal is considered to be one of Norway's most distinctive valley regions with rich cultural traditions. Sewing of traditional national costumes and silversmith work are also well maintained in the Setedal of today.

In summer, space in the harbours for pleasure craft is often at a premium. The harbour in Risør is no exception.

Fresh fish and seafood are also part of life in Southern Norway. Crab fishermen arrive with crabs they have just caught, while the boys prefer angling for tiddlers on the wharf.

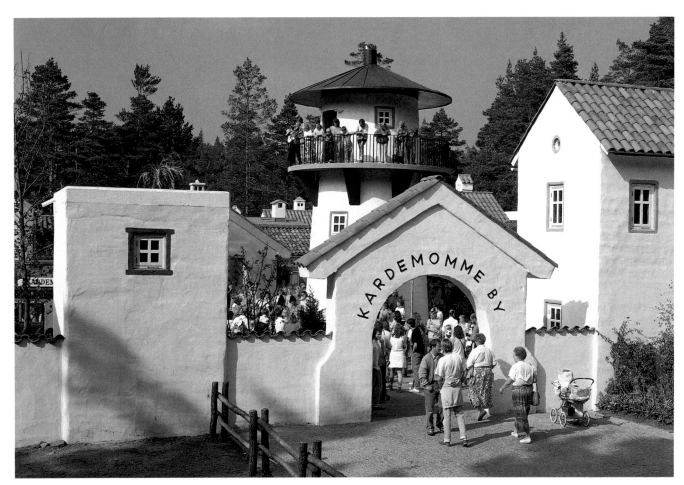

In Southern Norway,
Kristiansand Zoo is a popular
attraction for tourists and
locals alike. As well as seeing
animals from all over the
world, you can visit Torbjørn
Egner's Kardemomme By –
"Cardamom Town".

A refreshing dip in the tangy
sea feels good on a hot
summer's day.

Lindesnes Lighthouse, the southernmost point of the　➔
Norwegian mainland.

Western Norway

The Prekestolen ("Pulpit") mountain plateau, 600 m (1968 ft) above the Lysefjord in Ryfylke.

*V*estlandet's magnificent and changing scenery makes the region something very special. There are hardly any other places where one can experience the drama of the scenery and landscapes found here. The Vestland fjords extend for hundreds of kilometres into the mountain massif. Innermost in the fjord the idyll flourishes, racing with the natural forces, the waterfall runs and the rivers.

TRADITIONAL FOODS

Since days of old, food traditions in Norway have varied from region to region – depending on resources. The people of Western Norway prefer sheep's heads, "smalahove", when a feast is to be served. The sheep's heads have been through a long process before ending up on the banquet table; they are salted, then smoked and singed over an open flame.

Stavanger is the oil capital of Norway. Although oil operations have given the town vigorous economic growth and an international atmosphere, the beautiful old buildings of Stavanger have been preserved.

In a 30-year period, Norway has developed into one of the most important oil and gas nations in the world. The value of oil and gas pumped up from the Norwegian continental shelf amounts to about NOK 108,000 million per year in taxes and duties to the Norwegian state.

Solastrand is a popular beach for bathing.

The fruit blossom of Hardanger is a sight that is hard to forget.

The Hardanger national costume is considered one of the most beautiful in Norway.

In Stryn you can test your skiing skills – even in summer.

A glacier walk on the Jostedal glacier provides an experience that is quite out of the ordinary. The Jostedalen National Park has mountain peaks soaring to a height of 2083 metres (6832 ft).

← In Jølster, both folk music and national dress traditions are well preserved.

Borgund Stave Church (left), from
about 1150, is considered to be
the best preserved of the country's
29 stave churches.
Urnes Stave Church is the oldest
stave church in Norway, from
about 1100. It has been included
in UNESCO's World Heritage
List of cultural monuments most
worth preserving. The pictures
show details of the ornamentation
on the church.

The Briksdal glacier in Olden is a →
branch of the Jostedal glacier. It
was common to use a horse and
cart when tourists were to be
taken to the glacier.

The Flydalsjuvet gorge in Geiranger is
not for the fainthearted.

In 1904 Ålesund was ravaged by fire. About 800 houses burned
down, and the town had to be built up virtually from scratch. Today,
Ålesund stands out as a most picturesque town, where many of the
buildings are constructed in the Jugend style.

Bergen

HISTORICAL

Bergen was founded by Olav Kyrre in 1070. Its closeness to the sea and trade made Bergen Norway's largest and most important trading city up to the 1830s. The German members of the Hanseatic League left their mark on the city from the beginning of the 14th century until 1750, and turned the city into an international trade metropolis. Today, Bergen is Norway's next largest city, with flourishing cultural and industrial life. Bergen is also a centre for research and education.

*B*ergen has a beautiful location amid seven mountains. The city has a population of about 220,000, and the Coastal Express steamer route starts and ends here. Bryggen, the Fløibanen "tramway", the Fish Market and the Aquarium are popular sights.

SPRING'S GREAT MUSICAL ADVENTURE

The annual Bergen International Festival in May/June has become a major international cultural event. Here, world-renowned musicians, conductors and composers hold concerts. Edvard Grieg's home, Troldhaugen ("Troll's Hill") is one of the concert halls.

The Ulriksbanen cableway is one way to get to the top of Ulriken – one of the seven mountains surrounding Bergen

The penguins are popular with visitors to the Aquarium.

➡

Fløibanen is Bergen's only "tramway". If you take it to the top, you will get a magnificent view over Vågen and the city of Bergen.

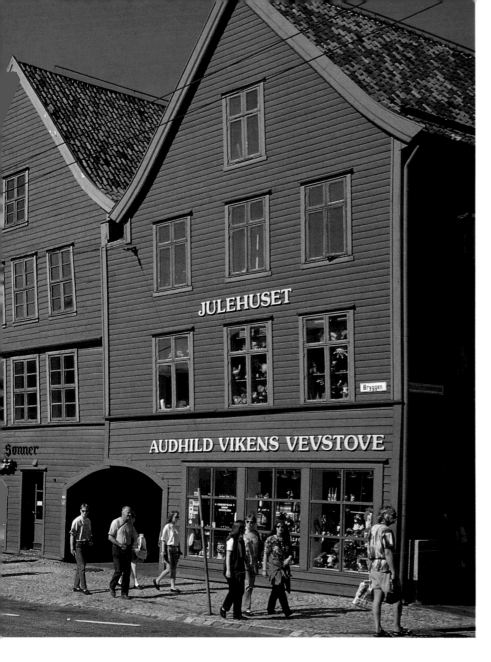

Bryggen is a reminder of the time that the German members of the Hanseatic League had great influence on the Bergen community.

The fish traders at the Bergen Fish Market have a hectic time when tourists stream in during the summer.

These "Buekorpsene" are an old tradition in Bergen. Until recently the bands have been for boys only, but now the girls of Bergen want to start their own.

← Bergen is well-known for its rainy climate. But, as we see, the people of Bergen know how to stay dry by dressing to suit the weather.

It is not surprising that the people of Bergen are proud of their city. Evening mood in Bergen, with Vågen in the foreground.

Central Norway

Rainbow over mountain lake at Dovre.

entral Norway is Norway in miniature. Within a limited area you will find sea and fjords, fertile agricultural areas and wild mountain landscapes. In historical times, central Norway was the hub of the country. Our first kings and chiefs lived here, while the region became the centre of the Norwegian church powers.

ELDORADO FOR SALMON FISHERMEN

As far as experiencing nature is concerned, central Norway has a great deal to offer. Among other things, the local salmon rivers are considered to be among the most attractive in the world. Since as early as the mid-19th century, salmon fishermen from Europe have sought out these rivers.

The mountain town of Røros is on UNESCO's World Heritage List of cultural monuments most worth preserving. It was the copper ore that provided the foundation for the development of the town 350 years ago. The church is built in the Baroque style, and was constructed in 1780.

Reindeer are attractive game for hunters in the Norwegian mountains.

The herd of musk oxen introduced at Dovre seems to be flourishing. Today the herd consists of 70 to 80 animals.

Tofte kongsgård, the King's estate in the municipality of Dovre, was a coaching station from medieval times.

The biting winter of central Norway makes great demands on the railways.

Moonlight over Dovrefjell.

Trollstigen is probably one of the most breathtaking examples of road engineering in Norway.

Rafting is also a way of getting around. In the steepest runs of the Driva river, the speed is nothing to complain about.

Cormorants abound on the coast of central Norway. →

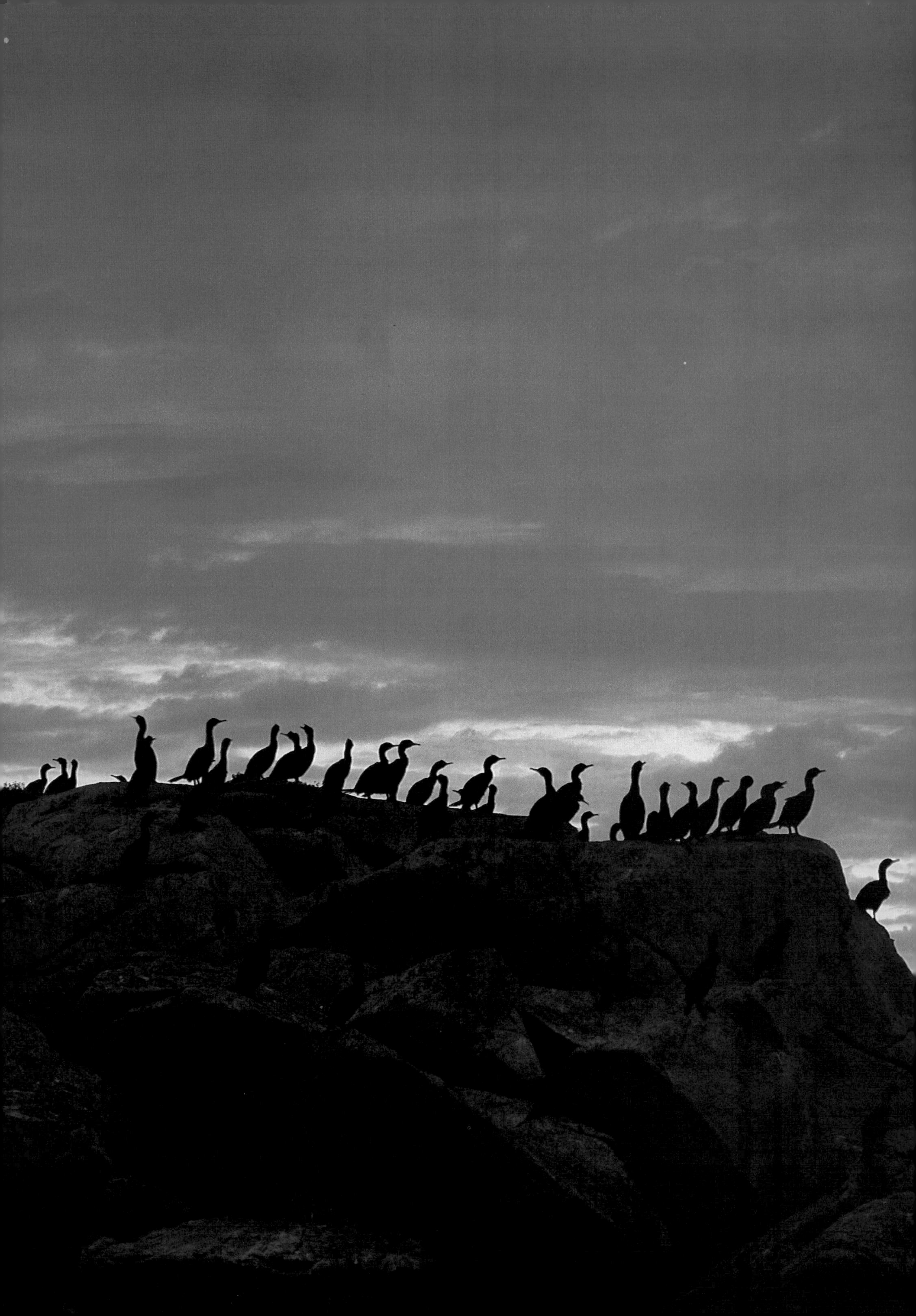

Trondheim

HISTORICAL

Norway's first capital. Trondheim was founded by the Viking king Olav Tryggvasson in 997. The greater Norwegian kingdom that extended from Kvitsjøen to North America was governed from Trondheim, or Nidaros as the city was called in the old days. The saga relates that it was from Nidaros that Leiv Eirikson sailed and eventually landed at Newfoundland in North America. After the fall of the canonized King Olav the Holy in the Battle of Stiklestad, Trondheim became the ecclesiastical centre of the country, and an international destination for pilgrims.

The mortal remains of King Olav the Holy were placed on the high altar in Nidaros Cathedral for nearly 500 years. In this period, pilgrims from the whole of Northern Europe travelled to Nidaros and the Olav shrine. Today there are about 400 St. Olav's churches in the world. In Trondheim, the day of the saint-king's death, July 29, is commemorated by the annual Olav Days in July/August.

LAND OF SAINT OLAV

Trondheim, the country's third largest city with a population of 140,000, is today a modern university and research city, and the business centre of central Norway. Trondheim is extremely rich in historical monuments, and it is regarded as one of Scandinavia's best preserved cities of wooden buildings.

In 1991, King Harald and Queen Sonja were blessed at the Nidaros Cathedral in Trondheim. The Royal Couple left the city from Ravnkloa. Ravnkloa is the city's fish market.

Trondheim's location between the river and the fjord made the city almost impregnable for hostile forces in the old days. This was probably one of the main reasons that the Viking king Olav Tryggvasson founded a trading centre here as early as 997. Out in the fjord is the island of Munkholmen.

Swimming at Munkholmen.

In summer, Trondheim's market square is a busy trading centre, where fruit and vegetables are the main products sold.

Nidaros Cathedral, Norway's national sanctuary, is the largest medieval building in Scandinavia. The church is built on the grave of the saint-king St. Olav, who died in the Battle of Stiklestad in 1030. In the Middle Ages, Trondheim was one of Europe's pilgrimage cities.

Detail from the row of sculptures on the western façade.

Trondheim's founder, Olav Tryggvasson, is portrayed in a statue in Trondheim's market square. The statue forms part of the world's largest sundial.

The Gamle Bybro (Old Town Bridge) with its "Gateway to Happiness" is a well-known feature of Trondheim's city profile.

Northern Norway

$\mathcal{N}$orthern Norway – the land of the Midnight Sun – includes the three counties of Nordland, Troms and Finnmark. The scenery of Northern Norway offers at least as many contrasts as the rest of the country – from Nordland's luxuriant and impressive coastal landscape to Finnmark's rugged and barren outer boundary with the inhospitable Barents Sea. The climate and nature have made their mark on the culture and way of life. When the sun returns

after a long, dark period in the middle of winter, a sun celebration is held in our two northernmost counties.

CODFISH: WEALTH FROM THE SEA

Lofoten is widely known for its fishing banks where cod arrive to spawn. In February/March, an amazing fishing season takes place, and hundreds of fishing boats stream in from all over coastal Norway.

Midnight sun at the Nykan bird rocks in Vesterålen.

It is hard to imagine more golden sand, or clearer water, than at this bathing beach in Lofoten.

At the old trading centre of Kjerringøy in Nordland, Knut Hamsun's well-known novel "Benoni og Rosa" was filmed as a television series.

The "Ice Cathedral" at Svartisen makes human beings seem tiny.

View from a boathouse in Lyngenfjord, Troms, on a sun winter's day.

➡

"Boat in the field". Nordland boat drawn up at the landing place near Tromsø.

Whale photo-safari outside Andøya attracts tourists from the whole world.

Fishing is the main industry for the Lofoten population.

*One of the great
experiences for passengers
on the Coastal Express is
the trip into the
Trollfjorden.*

*Leap through the air on the
Svolværgeita ("Svolvær Goat")
mountain in Svolvær, Lofoten.*

← *The puffin is a yearly visitor
at the bird rocks of Northern
Norway.*

Kirkeporten, the "Church Gate" at the North Cape.

Hammerfest is the oldest worlds northern-most city, with city status dating from 1789. The city introduced electric street lighting as early as 1891, making it one of the first cities in Northern Europe to get this kind of lighting.

→

The North Cape, Norway's last outpost bordering the Arctic Sea, at 70° 10' 21". The North Cape is one of the most visited tourist destinations in Norway. The midnight sun lasts from May 12 to August 1.

← The "Arctic Cathedral" – Tromsdalen Church in Tromsø – is an impressive sight.

The rock carvings of Alta – more than 5,000 years old, with 3,000 carvings altogether – were a sensation when they were discovered by chance in 1973. The field has been included in UNESCO's World Heritage List of cultural monuments most worth preserving.

Cotton grass, Finnmarksvidda.

Keeping reindeer is still an important livelihood for the Sami people today, just as it has been since time immemorial.

Svalbard

Svalbard is Norway's exotic outpost in the Arctic, and consists of five large and many smaller islands. Deep fjords and glacial valleys cut through the largest islands. The Svalbard soil is poor, but in the hectic summer season the vegetation almost explodes into a new and busy growth period. This provides abundant nourishment for the musk oxen that have been introduced and the indigenous Svalbard

reindeer, so that they can face a new, harsh Arctic winter.

REALM OF THE POLAR BEAR

Along the coast of Svalbard there are large colonies of seabirds, and on the drift ice around the group of islands there are relatively large numbers of polar bears and seals.

Longyearbyen is an active community with about 1,000 inhabitants.

At the innermost point of the fjord arm, the glacier meets the sea water.

Norway

MAP LEGEND

— Principal railway
— Principal road
⊙ City
○ Major town
• Small town, village
-·-·- National border
✈ Airport

North Cape
Honningsvåg
Gamvik
Kjøllefjord
Berlevåg
Båtsfjord
Vardø
Hammerfest
Tana bru
Vadsø
Kirkenes
Alta
Lakselv
Nordreisa
Karasjok
Tromsø
Skibotn
Bidjovagge
Andenes
Nordkjosbotn
Finnsnes
Bardufoss
Kautokeino
Sortland
Harstad
Stokkmarknes
Lødingen
Narvik
Leknes
Svolvær
Kjøpsvik
Reine
Nordfold
Værøy
Røst
Bodø
Fauske
Rognan
Glomfjord

Arctic Circle

Mo i Rana
Sandnessjøen
Korgen
Mosjøen
Hattfjelldal
Brønnøysund
Røssv.
Trofors
Rørvik
Namsos
Grong
Snåsav.
Snåsa
Steinkjer
Verdal
Levanger
Stjørdal
TRONDHEIM
Kristiansund
Orkanger
Surnadalsøra
Støren
Molde
Ulsberg
Aursund
Ålesund
Sunndalsøra
Åndalsnes
Oppdal
Røros
Ørsta
Stranda
Hjerkinn
Volda
Geiranger
Tynset
Stryn
Dombås
Alvdal
Florø
Byrkjelo
Lom
Femund
Vågå
Førde
Otta
Balestrand
Sogndal
Bygdin
Koppang
Lærdal
Årdal
Ringebu
Gudvangen
Flåm
Fagernes
Lillehammer
Rena
Voss
Geilo
Gol
Gjøvik
Elverum
BERGEN
Randsfj.
Hamar
Mjøsa
Kinsarvik
Jevnaker
Leirvik
Odda
Hønefoss
Kongsvinger
Haukeligrend
Rjukan
Tyrifj.
Haugesund
Kongsberg
OSLO
Notodden
Drammen
Seljord
Horten
STAVANGER
Tønsberg
Moss
Sandnes
Ålgård
Skien
Sarpsborg
Porsgrunn
Fredrikstad
Tonstad
Larvik
Sande-
Halden
Egersund
Evje
fjord
Risør
Flekkefjord
Tvedestrand
Farsund
Arendal
Mandal
Grimstad
Kristiansand

Svalbard
RUSSIA
FINLAND
SWEDEN
Island
Newcastle
Newcastle
Amsterdam
Hanstholm
Hirtshals
Fredrikshavn
Kiel
Göteborg/København
DENMARK

EUROPE

SVALBARD
ICELAND
TROMSØ
TRONDHEIM
SWEDEN
BERGEN
NORWAY
FINLAND
STAVANGER
OSLO
IRELAND
DENMARK
ESTONIA
UNITED
KINGDOM
LATVIA
NETHERLANDS
LITHUANIA
BELGIUM
GERMANY
POLAND
BELORUSSIA
LUXEM-
BURG
CZEK
REPUBLIC
FRANCE
SLOVAK
REPUBLIC
SWITZER-
LAND
AUSTRIA
MOLDOVA
PORTUGAL
SLOVENIA
HUNGARY
ANDORRA
KROATIA
ROMANIA
SPAIN
SAN
BOSNIA
MONACO
MARINO
HERZE-
YUGOSLAVIA
GOVINA
(Montenegro, Serbia)
ITALY
BULGARIA
ALBANIA
MACEDONIA
GREECE
TURKEY
MALTA

96

Text:

Svein Nic. Norberg

English translation: Margaret Forbes

Editors: Bjørn Østraat, Knut J. Lysklett, Ole P. Rørvik

Photo:

Knut Aune: page 94 bottom. Giulio Bolognesi: p.1, 2-3, 20-21, 22-23, 23 top, 49, 52 left, 52 bottom.
Kolbjørn Dekkerhus: p.7, 21 right, 29, 30-31, 32, 33 top, 34 top, 35, 44, 45, 46-47, 48, 55 right, 62 top, 67, 73 bottom.
Ole P. Rørvik: p.6, 8-9, 9 right, 11 bottom, 12-13, 14-15, 15top, 16 top, 18-19, 26-27, 34 bottom, 36-37,
38, 39, 42, 52, 52 top, 53, 54-55, 55 bottom, 56-57, 63 bottom, 66 bottom, 70-71, 72-73, 74, 75, 76-77,
78-79 top, 78 bottom, 80, 81, 82-83, 85, 86, 87, 88-89, 91, 94 top.
Angar: p.92-93. Espen Bratlie/Samfoto: p.15 middle. Finn Loftesnes: p.43 left. Willy Haraldsen: p.58-59.
Husmo-foto: p.40-41, Knudsens Fotosenter: p.10-11, 23n, 24-25, Kon-Tiki-museet: p.17 bottom.
Nasjonalgalleriet: p.16 bottom. Oldsakssamlingen: p.17 top. Ole Magnus Rapp: p.90. Scan-Foto: p.11 top, 15 bottom.
Kjell O. Storvik: p.84. Hanne Strager: p.83 right. Hans Strand: p.64-65. Robin Strand: p.50-51, 54 bottom.
Helge Sunde/Samfoto: p.66 top. Jon Arne Sæter: p.68-69, 78-79 bottom. Jørn Thomassen: p.93 right, 94 middle, 95.
Troldhaugen: p.51. Tore Wuttudal: p.33 bottom, 60-61, 63 top. Jon Østeng Hov: p.28, 62 bottom. Trond Aalde: p.43 right.
Thanks to Alsaker & Christiansen for the photo of sheep's heads, «smalahove» p.37,
and to C.F. Wesenberg for the photo of national costume from Setesdal p.31.
Cover: Terje Rakke , Bård Løken/Samfoto (background photo)
Back page: Stein P. Aasheim (mountain climber), Kolbjørn Dekkerhus, Ole P. Rørvik, Jørn Thomassen (polar bear)
Flyleaf: Geir Olaf Gjerden, Giulio Bolognesi, Ole P. Rørvik.

Layout and typography: Reklamebyrået Cicignon. *Repro:* Trondheim Repro. *Print:* Lade Offset.